Land of the Commonwealth

A Portrait of the Conserved Landscapes of Massachusetts

PHOTOGRAPHY BY RICHARD CHEEK

FOREWORD BY JOHN UPDIKE

INTRODUCTION BY ROBERT E. COOK

TEXT BY LIBBY OLA HOPKINS

AFTERWORD BY FREDERIC WINTHROP

Published by The Trustees of Reservations

Distributed by the University of Massachusetts Press

DEDICATED TO THOSE

WHO HAVE WORKED TIRELESSLY

TO PRESERVE THE LANDSCAPE

HERITAGE OF MASSACHUSETTS

First Printing

Copyright © 2000 by The Trustees of Reservations
All photographs copyright © 2000 by Richard Cheek

ISBN 1-55849-265-8

Library of Congress Number
00-131606

Editing, Project Management, and Captions: Michael Triff
Publishing Consultant: Steve Pekich
Design: Julia Sedykh Design
Printed and bound in Tokyo, Japan, by Dai Nippon, Inc.

Published by The Trustees of Reservations
572 Essex Street, Beverly, MA 01915
Tel: (978) 921-1944
www.thetrustees.org

Distributed by the University of Massachusetts Press
P.O. Box 429, Amherst, MA 01004
Tel: (413) 545-2219
www.umass.edu/umpress

*Captions for pages 1 through 14 appear in order
below. Properties of The Trustees of Reservations are
distinguished by green type.*

Ipswich
CRANE BEACH, THE CRANE ESTATE
Witnessed by few, a snow-covered dune with
its frozen mounds of tufted beach grass makes a
puzzling portraiture of a barrier beach, a landscape
typically associated with the heat of summer.

Williamstown
FIELD FARM
As the autumn sun sets over Field Farm, nearby
Mount Greylock casts its massive shadow down
the steep face of the Taconics and over the fertile
valley's cornfields, hayfields, and pastures.

Ipswich
CASTLE HILL, THE CRANE ESTATE
An avenue of spruce trees splits the morning sun
into alternating bands of light and shade across
Castle Hill's snow-encrusted Grand Allee.

Petersham
BROOKS WOODLAND PRESERVE
Protagonists in the story of this ever-changing
landscape, beavers complete a new lodge along a
slow-flowing section of the East Branch of the
Swift River.

Petersham
SWIFT RIVER RESERVATION
Twiggy black birch trees frantically colonize a
patch of the woodland floor momentarily illuminated by an opening in the forest canopy.

Salem Bay
MISERY ISLANDS
Hay-scented ferns and lichen lay claim to the
overgrown stone foundations of former cottages
which once made Great Misery Island a popular
summer colony.

Provincetown
CAPE COD NATIONAL SEASHORE
In October 1849, during the first of his four
sojourns to Cape Cod, Henry David Thoreau con-
ceived the structure and narrative for his book
Cape Cod. He concluded his historic hike near Race
Point Beach, the outermost edge of this remarkable coastal landscape.

Chesterfield
CHESTERFIELD GORGE
Sections of the Westfield River are participating
sites in an Atlantic Salmon re-population program designed to return the wild salmon to the
Connecticut River and its tributaries. In spring,
salmon eggs are stocked in the river's pools at
Chesterfield Gorge.

CONTENTS

The success of any attempt to portray the beauty, breadth, and variety of the Commonwealth's vast panoply of protected landscapes depends upon the generosity of many individuals who are willing to share their time, energy, money, knowledge, and expertise. This book has benefited from many such contributors, each of whom deserves much more than the cursory note of thanks that follows.

Tatiana Bezamat must come first. Her suggestion for a modest picture book about Castle Hill led to my counterproposal for a portrait of all the major reservations belonging to The Trustees of Reservations, a publication which she promptly and graciously agreed to support by underwriting the photography and raising additional funds.

Convinced of the wisdom of the project, Executive Director Fred Winthrop got things started by introducing me to board members and to departmental directors at headquarters: John Coleman, Dick Howe, Lisa McFadden, and Ann Powell. Their enthusiastic advice and assistance proved to be essential during the photography.

Wes Ward, Director of Land Conservation, also stepped into the picture, first, to suggest looking beyond The Trustees of Reservations' borders to include significant landscapes conserved by other organizations, private and public, and second, to share his passion for every one of the fifty-two types of Massachusetts landscapes he identified at my request.

Out in the field, I enjoyed the clear trails, enhanced vistas, and superb guidance provided by regional directors Wayne Mitton, Tom Foster, Chris Kennedy, Dick O'Brien, Stan Piatczyc, and his successor, Steve McMahon, and by individual site superintendents and staff specialists including Mark Baer, Mark Bailey, Dave Belcher, Dick Bellevue, Andy Bernardy, Diane Boretos, Jim Caffrey, Greg Chanis, Jean and Sean Cowhig, "Emo" DeWitt, Chris Egan, Bill Girardi, Paul Gryzbowski, Hillary Hamilton, Marcel LaJeunesse, Bob Murray, Peter Pinciaro, Don Reid, Dave Rimmer, Lillabeth Wies, and Al Yalenezian. The most fleeting moments recorded in this book, from icy stalagmites in a graphite mine to a new beaver lodge in a freshly flooded glade, are there only because someone else's keen eye alerted me to their presence.

I am also grateful to the five authors whose eloquence amplifies our understanding and appreciation of the Commonwealth's conserved landscapes: John Updike, Bob Cook, Libby Hopkins, Michael Triff, and Fred Winthrop.

Always ready to offer calm, expert advice whenever a problem arose, publishing consultant Steve Pekich was crucial to the project. He led us to our splendid book designer, Julia Sedykh, whose crisp, dynamic layout highlights the same graphic features in the landscape that inspired the photographs. It has also been a privilege to be associated with Bruce Wilcox, Director of the University of Massachusetts Press, who made many welcome suggestions regarding the basic and finer points of publishing.

Any publishing endeavor that tries to cover so much territory needs an editor to sharpen the text and organize its presentation, a watchdog to keep the project afloat financially, and a manager to oversee design and production. As Director of Communications and Marketing for The Trustees of Reservations since 1997, Michael Triff has performed these multiple tasks with skill and aplomb. For his next act, he will make this book fly off the shelf.

And, finally, I thank my wife, Betsy, and my son, Dan, for helping me to stay on the trail for seven years until the book was finished.

RICHARD CHEEK

Those of us who have lived in Ipswich know the moment when Argilla Road, heading toward Crane Beach, slips its sheath of roadside houses and trees and the view on the right becomes an immense one of salt marshes and, beyond their grassy flat extent, sand dunes and the horizon of the ocean. This is open space, the kind that The Trustees of Reservations has been preserving in Massachusetts since 1891. The Trustees' holdings in Ipswich are especially vast and varied—nearly three thousand acres, including miles of spectacular white sand beach, a number of hills, several sizable islands, and a fifty-nine-room mansion with outbuildings, not to mention, on the other side of town, a nearly one thousand-acre working farm. The more than eighty properties under the protection of The Trustees of Reservations in the Commonwealth of Massachusetts stretch from the Coskata-Coatue Wildlife Refuge on Nantucket Island to Field Farm in the Berkshires. The view from my present house in Beverly includes Great and Little Misery Islands, whose pleasantly unpopulated condition was recently assured by The Trustees of Reservations' acquisition of the last three acres still in private hands.

If Massachusetts, one of the longest-settled and most populous of the states, remains one of the most livable, one reason is the formation, over a century ago, of a group of citizens whose public spirit dedicated itself to the acquisition of "bits of scenery" as "country parks" for the growing and crowded masses of greater Boston. The quoted phrases are from the fluent pen of Charles Eliot, the son of Harvard professor (and later president) Charles William Eliot. Young Eliot apprenticed for two years in the Brookline office of Frederick Law Olmsted and then traveled through parts of Europe studying public parks, gardens, and great private estates. At the age of twenty-seven, he opened an office in Boston at the corner of Beacon and Park Streets as a landscape architect. Writing to the periodical *Garden and Forest* in 1890, he observed that close to the metropolis remained "several bits of scenery which possess uncommon beauty and more than usual refreshing power." He cited the narrows of the Charles River in Sherborn, which became in 1897 one of the first acquisitions of The Trustees of Reservations, an organization "empowered by the State," as Eliot proposed, "to hold small and well-distributed parcels of land free of taxes, just as the Public Library holds books and the Art Museum pictures—for the use and enjoyment of the public." Eliot died at the young age of thirty-seven, but his noble idea flourished, along with his brain child, the first private statewide organization in the country devoted to the preservation of open space—"surviving fragments," as he wrote, "of the primitive wilderness of New England."

Not many of the reserved properties are "primitive wilderness"; they include the Great House at Castle Hill, Naumkeag, the Old Manse, Long Hill, as well as a number of other domiciles, gardens, and working farms. But each holding, it could be said, rescues a certain moment of landscape from the predations of unbridled development. Since we are all part of the press of population that would replace wilderness with human habitations, industry, and commerce—the Native Americans cleared fields and erected dwellings, and even the seemingly virgin salt marshes have been trenched and drained—it would seem paradoxical to resist, by means of advanced organization and substantial funds, the triumph of our own species over the surface of the earth. An asphalt parking lot is, in a sense, as natural as a lava spill, and a factory, as a honeycomb. The nineteenth-century mills of Lowell have become themselves the objects of preservation efforts, their beauty and splendor revealed as their utility subsides.

The first McDonald's, in Des Plaines, Illinois, is now a piously visited museum. Still, nature without man, or with selective human refinements modestly added to a natural effect, possesses, in Eliot's phrase, a "refreshing power."

Nature has its balances, and the human race is not so omnipotent as to avoid the penalties of a persisting imbalance. Deforestation brings floods, overgrazing produces deserts. The Trustees of Reservations was founded in an era that lacked the word "ecology" and that knew far less than our own about the environmental value of lands too wet for houses or crops, or the role that plants' emission of oxygen plays in our atmosphere. What at first seems waste in nature turns out, often, to be essential. An efficient inefficiency presides above the workings of the planet in its full range of flora and fauna, of water and air and permeable soil. We belong to this lavish dispensation, an animal evolved on the East African grassland, a hunter and harvester among many, accustomed to wide spaces and small tribes. "I love a broad margin to my life," Henry David Thoreau wrote in *Walden* and, in his journals, "the savage in man is never quite eradicated."

The New England conscience, brought by the Puritans to a rocky, resistant terrain, is prone to a certain parsimony with regard to its natural inheritance. Thoreau's essay "Walking" begins, "I wish to speak a word for Nature, for absolute freedom and wildness, as contrasted with a freedom and culture merely civil,—to regard man as an inhabitant, or a part and parcel of Nature, rather than a member of society." Thoreau's New England had still enough untrammeled spaces in it—Cape Cod, in his day, provided a walk on the wild side and not a mile-long traffic jam on Route 6—for him to feel an opposition between nature and society. One could escape from one into the other. His little Walden wilderness, never as isolated as his great book suggests, is now a heavily used suburban preserve.

Having endured utopian visions of Bauhausian "machines for living" and towering apartment blocks where greenery is kept like a lapdog and all neighborhood scale is lost, we can see that some protected aboriginal nature is essential for social health. The town of Ipswich, for instance, benefits as a whole—acquires a communal *panache*—from the presence within it of upland, beaches, dunes, and marshes kept relatively pristine. Charles Eliot's perception that spaces uncluttered by human enterprise feed our spiritual and physical well-being was not unique; such a perception lay at the heart of romantic poetry and was extended by ecstatics like John Muir, who chose for the motto of the Wilderness Society Thoreau's remark "In wildness is the preservation of the world." Muir provided the theological paraphrase "In God's wildness lies the hope of the world—the great fresh, unblighted, unredeemed wilderness."

The Trustees of Reservations, without much rhetoric, but with much patient study and quiet generosity, has acquired and maintains for our Commonwealth more than eighty tracts of land, large and small, beautifully portrayed herein by the photographs of Richard Cheek. Nature's gifts have been seconded by the gifts of human benefactors and workers committed to the vision of a planet shared among all its life forms, an Eden under human stewardship.

JOHN UPDIKE
Beverly Farms, Massachusetts

To penetrate the popular psyche, conservation has frequently opted to sound a call to arms with dire predictions of disaster and disturbing images of our dominant, exploitative relationship with nature. One thinks most readily of Rachel Carson's *Silent Spring,* which grew out of a letter sent to the author by a friend decrying the horrible deaths of songbirds following aerial spraying of DDT in Duxbury, Massachusetts. Combined with an emerging public understanding of the science of ecology, Carson's eloquent writing launched a national revolution in environmental awareness and advocacy. The rhetoric of conservation has often been suffused with pessimism grounded in real ecological crisis: the extinction of rare and endangered species, the contamination of groundwater, clear-cutting of forests, and global alteration of the climate. These calamities seldom make attractive images, but their shock value has provided fuel for the environmental movement in the United States and around the world.

Yet, paradoxically, here is a large-scale photographic book, published by one of the nation's oldest conservation organizations, that forthrightly celebrates, through strikingly beautiful photographs, a great many examples of Massachusetts' most cherished landscapes. Is this tantamount to activism? I think so. Conservation in the modern age has learned that its aims can also be well served by success. However, the accomplishments so beautifully depicted in this book by no means suggest that the whole job has been done. Rather, this book signals the equally pressing and even more daunting work ahead.

Through most of its 109 years, The Trustees of Reservations has focused its work on the preservation of landscapes of exceptional scenic and historic value. As our knowledge of natural systems and of the consequences of our own seemingly boundless consumption of resources deepens, ecological values, such as biological diversity, have necessarily assumed a position of high priority among the goals of conservation. Since 1985, these have been specifically incorporated into the stated mission of The Trustees of Reservations.

Seen in this light, Richard Cheek's photographs represent, in a highly aesthetic way, the hidden worlds of processes, connections, and consequences that, in violated landscapes, are lost. We know that, beyond the focus of even Cheek's remarkable lens, layers upon layers of detail and complexity remain invisible. Each of these seemingly perfect landscapes, whether designed by a landscape architect, cultivated by a farmer, managed by a forester, or left to its own natural devices, is a real place literally crawling and sprouting with life.

While we can imagine the unseen ecologies in each of these settings, I believe that these images also call to mind an older, often overlooked, notion—one that emphasizes our spiritually, physically, and mentally therapeutic relationship with nature. It arose, as John Updike alludes to in his Foreword, in the mid-nineteenth century and was a guiding influence on Charles Eliot and the founders of The Trustees of Reservations long before conservation became a popular cause. I think this notion underscores the lasting cultural significance of this movement's accomplishments during at least the past hundred years.

In 1889, when Charles Eliot first called on "generous men and women" to form an association empowered to acquire "fine and strongly characterized works of Nature," his larger vision sought the preservation of "the finest bits of natural scenery near Boston . . . for the enjoyment of the public . . . as an antidote to the poisonous struggling and excitement of city life." "The rich," Eliot wrote, "satisfy these desires by fleeing from town at certain seasons, but the needs of the more poor can only be met by the preservation of surviving fragments of New England's wilderness."

Eliot shared with his mentor, Frederick Law Olmsted, the conviction that the experience of scenic beauty had direct, health-related benefits for the body and the mind. As expressed by Olmsted in an 1865 report written to the California legislature commending the preservation of Yosemite Valley,

> The enjoyment of scenery employs the mind without fatigue and yet it exercises it; tranquilizes it and yet enlivens it; and thus, through the influence of the mind over the body, gives the effect of refreshing rest and reinvigoration of the whole system ... The want of such occasional recreation ... results in ... mental and nervous excitability, moroseness, melancholy or irascibility, incapacitating the subject for the proper exercise of the intellectual and moral forces.

For Olmsted and Eliot, the preservation of landscapes was as much about the mental and spiritual health of human beings as it was about the conservation of scenery, history, and natural systems. Belief in the restorative powers of nature was, in Olmsted and Eliot's day, a relatively new idea in America, inspired by eighteenth-century European romantics and reaching its most eloquent expression in the Transcendental writings of Ralph Waldo Emerson and Henry David Thoreau. For the first time in this country, the colonial fear of—and impulse to subjugate—the wild was transformed into a humanistic reverence for the spiritual power of nature and its capacity to develop moral character in men and women of all classes and callings.

This philosophical shift was reinforced by growing antipathy toward the appalling conditions of the nineteenth-century city and their consequences for the great mass of immigrants struggling to survive in these burgeoning centers of commerce. Between 1790 and 1880, the urban population of Boston increased from 18,000 to 362,000. This expansion was largely made up of laborers in the mills and factories who stoked the Industrial Revolution. Tragically, the population explosion quickly overwhelmed Boston's municipal infrastructure, including waterworks, sewage treatment, and garbage collection. Sanitary conditions in the streets, back yards, and alleys were dreadful, and sources of drinking water shared common ground with the leaching fields of privies and the graveyards of nearby churches.

Not surprisingly, the greatest fear of city dwellers was suffering and death brought on by disease. Before the development of germ theory at the end of the century, epidemics were believed to be caused by miasmas or noxious gases and odors arising from the ground. In urban areas, these "putrid exhalations" led to the contagious spread of such scourges as smallpox, cholera, diphtheria, and yellow fever, especially among the crowded tenements of the poorer districts of the city. By contrast, the country—with fresh breezes, open meadows and great stands of trees—could effectively dissipate these miasmas and relax the mind through the enjoyment of scenic beauty.

The preservation of rural scenery was fundamentally a democratic and humanitarian obligation similar in its importance and purpose to the urban reform movements of their day. After the turn of the twentieth century, the idea of scenic preservation lost much of its ideological connection to public health and concern for the welfare of the urban poor. The growth of the national park system, especially in the western United States, created a strong alliance between conservation and the economics of recreational tourism. Today, especially, scenic enjoyment implies a personal, leisurely pleasure without much connotation of greater moral purpose or therapeutic value.

Perhaps our current ideas about scenic value have become too narrow, invoking associations with rugged topography, long panoramas to distant hills, or coastal views of windswept dunes. The scale is grand, the key qualification is visual appeal, and the reward is a momentary sense of satisfaction in seeing to the horizon.

While I enjoy great vistas of forested slopes or rocky crags, I also take considerable delight in scenes that are extremely small, such as one finds on the forest floor. It may be a long-ago fallen tree that has become home to a thriving community of brightly colored mosses and oddly shaped fungi; such rotting logs hold special places in my memory. Or one can recall the sudden discovery, deep in a second-growth forest, of the straight line of a stone wall with all of its boulders growing gardens of textured lichens.

We grow up knowing the land through our eyes. Our accumulated experience outdoors creates a special and highly meaningful relationship between person and place, rooted in a sense of belonging that leads us to deeper feelings of stewardship about the land around us.

But these are prosperous times in Massachusetts, and land is a legal commodity. Population continues to rise, and the market gives us what we want: homes, shopping centers, malls, and expanding transportation and communication networks. Modern-day society threatens our everyday landscape: farmlands, large tracts of second-growth forest, nearby watersheds of ponds and rivers, and the greatly underappreciated greenswards that track our rural roads.

To quote Walt Kelly's immortal words in *Pogo*, "We have met the enemy, and he is us," but how do we engage these powerful forces of our own human striving for security, comfort, and abundance?

In the spirit of Charles Eliot, I would return to a more humble, egalitarian notion of conservation, one that recognizes the diverse ways people value the landscape and one that acknowledges its power to move and shape us. Through a renewed appreciation for all landscape values—scenic, historic, and ecological—and, moreover, for the healthy influence that land has on our lives, we may embark on a more symbiotic relationship with the land.

Herein lies the challenge for The Trustees of Reservations and other Massachusetts conservation groups in the years ahead: to instill in an increasingly urban and suburban population a sense of community and a stewardship ethic for the land, one of shared responsibility for saving the remaining special places—along with their essential connections and settings—that are so vital to our collective well-being. *Land of the Commonwealth* gives us a glorious beginning to a new era of conservation work.

ROBERT E. COOK
Director, Arnold Arboretum of Harvard University

Hingham
WORLD'S END
Enjoyed from the crest of Planter's Hill,
the summer solstice sunset over the City of
Boston and its harbor marks the end of the
longest day of the year.

Greater Boston and the Southeast

Spreading outward from the heart of Boston, a series of gardens and green spaces offers respite from an increasingly busy landscape of city and suburbs. Beneath skyscrapers and towers stand old markets, meeting houses, and cemeteries—many preserved as public spaces—that attest to the Commonwealth's early days as a prosperous and cantankerous colony. Offshore, the harbor islands protect a Civil War fort and acres of marine habitat offering the slower pace of the daily tides. Amid the buildings, highways, and crooked back streets of the city lies a patchwork of green. Here is the country's largest urban network of public gardens and parks, linked and landscaped with walkways, ponds, stone bridges, and sculptures. Here, too, are private gardens, overflowing with flowers and tomatoes, basil, and beans.

To the west and north of the city lie the quiet ponds, rivers, and woodlands that inspired Emerson, Thoreau, and Hawthorne. Winding along its 80-mile course to the sea, the Charles River is fringed here and there with broad freshwater marshes and wooded knolls of hemlock and beech.

To the south, the city and suburbs gradually lead to a gently rolling terrain of oak-hickory forest with pitch pine barrens, scattered kettle hole ponds, and Atlantic white cedar swamps. The coast is less crowded here, from the fingers and coves of Buzzards Bay to the marshes and flats of Duxbury Bay, where the air rings with the chatter of gulls and terns. The region's tidal rivers and sheltered inlets and channels were vital to early industries of shipbuilding, fishing, whaling, and textile manufacturing. Now, among growing towns, the land sustains small farms, vineyards, and abundant cranberry bogs. Beyond the farms, unique coastal plain ponds are home to rare wildflowers, turtles, and dragonflies, where tended gardens give way to wild ones.

Boston
ESPLANADE
Bordering the banks of the Charles River for several miles, the Esplanade offers outdoor recreation for thousands of people.

Medfield
SHATTUCK RESERVATION
As it flows through the Great Marsh, the Charles River forms a narrow, twisting ribbon of water bordered by broad, lush flood plains.

Boston
PUBLIC GARDEN
Towering trees, clipped topiary shrubs, statuary, and profuse plantings of flowering bulbs and annuals make this, the nation's first public botanical garden, one of Boston's most celebrated open spaces.

Concord

HUTCHINS FARM ▶

Small market gardens retain the traditional rural character of many towns around Boston. At the same time, they supply fresh, often organically grown vegetables. This market garden is protected by a conservation restriction, ensuring that the land will never be developed and will always be used for agriculture.

Boston

BOSTON COMMON

In 1634, the townspeople of Boston paid £30 to purchase the 44-acre Boston Common for military training and grazing cattle. In the 18th century, it was the site of gallows; in the 19th century, football games; and today, a pleasure park for local residents and visitors to Boston.

Boston

VICTORY GARDENS

The tiny plots of land comprising the so-called Victory Gardens were established during the second World War to help nearby residents overcome shortages in available fresh vegetables. Today, cultivated for both productive and aesthetic tastes, these plots are leased annually from the City of Boston.

Boston Harbor
GEORGES ISLAND
Managed through a public-private partnership,
the Boston Harbor Islands National Recreation
Area comprises thirty islands including Georges
Island, where the remains of Fort Warren pre-
serve the former prison home of Confederate
soldiers captured during the Civil War.

Concord
MINUTE MAN NATIONAL
HISTORICAL PARK
The North Bridge marks the site of an early
trestle bridge at which colonial militia men
repelled an attack by British soldiers and sent
them in retreat, thus firing "the shot heard
'round the world" and setting off the American
Revolution.

Cambridge
MOUNT AUBURN CEMETERY
Founded in 1831, Mount Auburn is the country's
oldest garden cemetery. Its many thousands
of graves are scattered across one hundred sev-
enty-five acres of landscaped grounds significant
for their history, sculpture, architecture, design,
horticulture, and wildlife.

Wellesley
ITALIAN TOPIARY GARDEN ▶
First laid out and planted in the 1850s, the
Italian Topiary Garden on the shores of Lake
Waban was the first topiary garden created
in America. At its height, it contained two
hundred fanciful topiary specimens of native
hardy conifers. Today, some fifty specimens are
meticulously maintained by the Hunnewell
family, who placed a conservation restriction
on the garden.

Jamaica Plain
ARNOLD ARBORETUM
With the continent's largest collection
of hardy trees, shrubs, and vines, the Arnold
Arboretum is arguably North America's
preeminent arboretum and center for plant
science research and education. Frederick Law
Olmsted incorporated the Arboretum into
the Emerald Necklace as one of its nine parks.

Boston
BACK BAY FENS
Viewed through the arch of the Boylston Street
Bridge, the Back Bay Fens remind us that Boston
was once an upland peninsula within the tidal
estuary of the Charles River. During Boston's
great land fill operation of the early 19th century,
35-car trains ran twenty-four hours a day for
thirty years transporting sand and gravel from
the west and depositing it into the Back Bay.

Carlisle and Concord
ESTABROOK WOODS
Batemans Pond lies near the heart of historic
Estabrook Woods, five square miles of protected
woodlands which have been conserved by a
remarkable partnership of individual landowners, conservation organizations, towns, and
private institutions.

Concord
WALDEN POND
The great 19th-century iconoclast Henry David
Thoreau recorded in *Walden* his toils, pleasures,
and philosophies on life while living in a cabin
he built in the woods surrounding this deep
kettle pond, now a popular public swimming
hole.

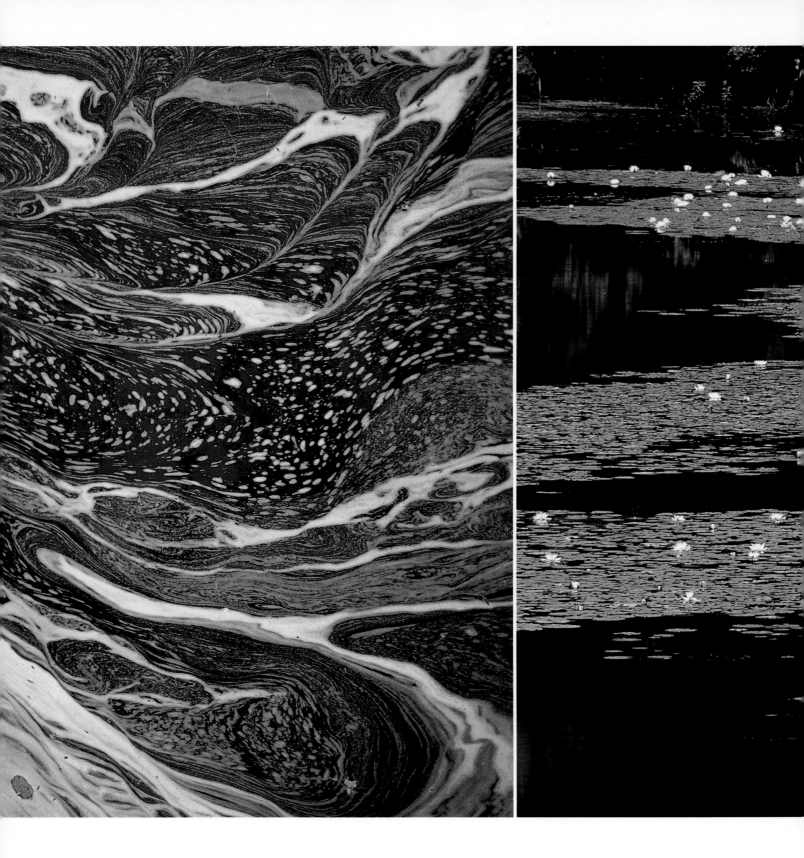

Needham and Newton
HEMLOCK GORGE
The waters of the Charles River foam at the Silk
Mill Dam spillway just below Hemlock Gorge.
In 1895, this 23-acre woodland became one
of the first properties to be incorporated into
the then-new Metropolitan Park System, the
first regional organization of public open space
in the United States.

Dover
NOANET WOODLANDS
Around 1815, Noanet Brook was dammed to
form a series of four small mill ponds to power
the forges of the Dover Union Iron Company.
Today, festooned with islands of white-flowered
water lilies, these ponds are part of a vast suburban area of conserved woodland.

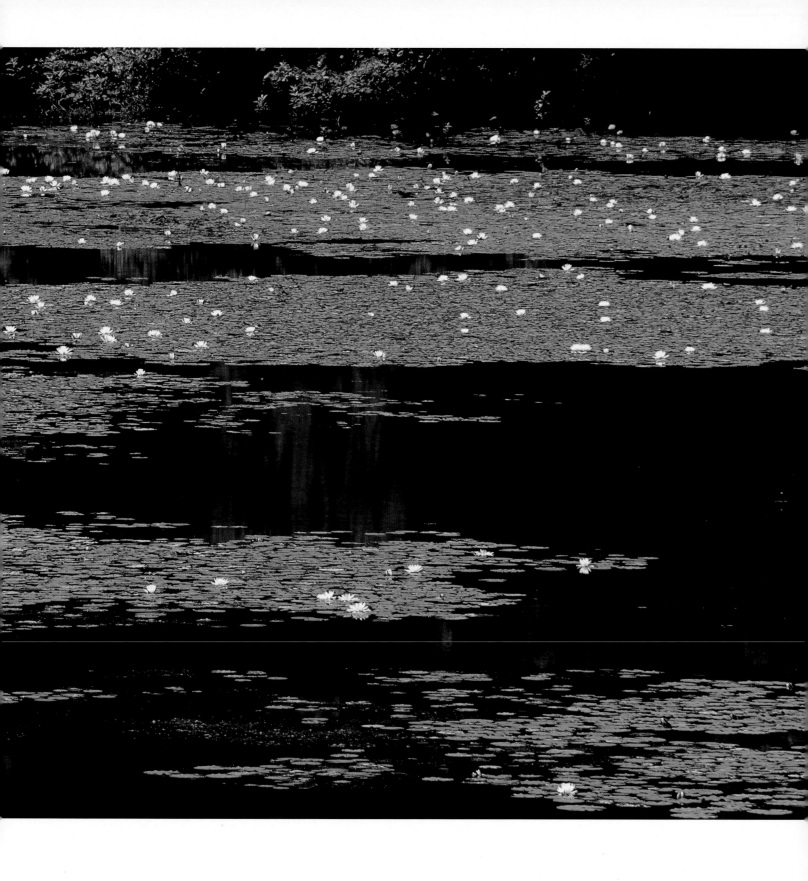

Concord
THE OLD MANSE
While living in this colonial parsonage, Ralph
Waldo Emerson drafted his essay "Nature," and
Nathaniel Hawthorne published *Mosses from
an Old Manse*. Buried in deep snow, the Old
Manse still evokes an impression of what the
landscape may have looked like in those days.

Norwell

NORRIS RESERVATION

Though long gone, shipyards once operated
along this tidal section of the North River.
Seemingly inexhaustible forests of oak, pine,
and larch were used to build over one thousand
sailing ships between 1678 and 1871. Today,
canoes and kayaks are the most common
vessels gracing the river.

Cohasset and Hingham
WHITNEY AND THAYER WOODS
Boulders emerge from the woodland floor. Many have been cleverly named, including "Ode's Den," named after a man who sheltered here in 1828 after losing his home.

Sherborn
ROCKY NARROWS
Heart-shaped leaves of Canada mayflower and runners of partridge-berry.

Canton
THE ELEANOR CABOT BRADLEY ESTATE
A gentle foot trail leads to a secluded dell in the woodland, one of the many landscape features of this former gentleman's farm which includes, around the main house, a walled kitchen garden, formal flower garden, sweeping lawns, fields, and pastures.

Brookline
FAIRSTED

At the peak of his career in 1883, Frederick Law Olmsted moved his landscape architecture firm from New York to Brookline to continue his work on Boston's Emerald Necklace. The house in which he lived and worked during the final seventeen years of his life is now a museum dedicated to interpreting the scope and genius of his work.

Boston and Brookline
RIVERWAY ▶

This section of the brackish, mosquito-infested Muddy River was re-channeled and its banks landscaped to represent a natural river valley untouched by development, forming one of the last links in Frederick Law Olmsted's Emerald Necklace.

Hingham
WORLD'S END
Tree-lined carriage roads laid out between 1886 and 1900 are all that remain of a planned 163-house community designed by Frederick Law Olmsted. In 1967, more than $450,000 was raised from 1,800 South Shore residents to ensure that the dramatic coastal drumlins that form World's End would be set aside as public open space.

HALIBUT POINT RESERVATION

The shifting beaches along the North Shore's Atlantic seaboard give way to unyielding rocky bluffs which emerge from below the ocean floor to form Cape Ann. The dramatic surf of these headlands becomes even more sensational when ocean storms deliver great whitecaps to the coastline.

Northeast Massachusetts

The Merrimack River and Cape Ann's rocky coast encompass a region of harbor towns and factory cities, designed estates and natural marshes that reflect the rise and fall of tides and fortunes. Inland from the rocky bluffs and forested headlands of Cape Ann's coast and islands, a gently rolling coastal plain, broken by occasional low hills, is green with a mixed oak-white pine forest with scattered red maple swamps and boulders left by the glacier. From the hills, rivers great and small—the Merrimack, Shawsheen, Parker, and Ipswich—meander toward the sea where they flow into broad estuaries. One mosaic of salt marsh, freshwater and brackish tidal marshes, and barrier beach forms the largest coastal marsh system in New England, covering 25,000 acres from Essex Bay to the Merrimack River. This prime habitat is home and resting place for birds and other wildlife, including plovers and tern, herons and egrets, and harriers that float over the marsh in search of prey.

The rocky coast's natural harbors encouraged a fishing tradition that survives in Gloucester. Early fishing fleets harvested cod from rich offshore banks. Coastal schooners were built here, and merchant trading grew, earning fortunes for some whose homes, estates, and gardens still stand overlooking the sea.

Upstream on the Merrimack River in Lowell and Lawrence, long mill buildings hug the river, source of the water that first ran the spindles and looms of a New England textile industry in the 1820s—the start of the country's Industrial Revolution. Today, the mills are part of historic districts and heritage parks. From the cities, busy highways lead to quiet back roads that wander through woods and small patches of farmland. Tilled fields, alfalfa meadows, horse pastures, and barns offer both views of a life lived off the land and the sweet aroma of new-mown hay.

Ipswich

CRANE BEACH, THE CRANE ESTATE

An unspoiled beach, dunes, and maritime forest make this one of New England's most picturesque—and popular—coastal landscapes. Stewardship of this barrier beach involves protecting habitats for plants, invertebrates, mammals, birds, shellfish, and finfish and, at the same time, providing access for the 200,000 visitors who flock here each year.

Ipswich
CASTLE HILL, THE CRANE ESTATE
Chicago plumbing tycoon Richard T. Crane, Jr.,
purchased Castle Hill in 1910 as a summer
estate for his family. David Adler designed
the 59-room Great House in the style of the
great country seats of England, and Arthur
Shurcliff devised the Grand Allee, a grassy,
spruce-lined mall connecting the Great House
to a precipice overlooking Crane Beach.

Essex and Ipswich
THE CRANE ESTATE
Viewed at sunset across Ipswich Bay from
Annisquam Light in Gloucester, Castle Hill, four-
mile-long Crane Beach, and the assorted islands
of the Crane Wildlife Refuge form a thin, back-
lit sliver on the horizon.

Manchester-by-the-Sea
COOLIDGE RESERVATION ▶
Enticing and invasive, beautiful magenta
spikes of blooming Purple Loosestrife (*Lythrum
salicaria*) cover the banks of Clarke Pond. This
aggressive, exotic species is rapidly spreading
across the landscape, displacing native plants,
and presenting a major threat to the ecological
integrity of many freshwater wetland habitats.

Hamilton and Ipswich

APPLETON FARMS

Established in 1638 as a land grant to
Samuel Appleton, Appleton Farms is one
of the oldest continuously operating farms
in America. Its grassy fields are grazed by
livestock, its fertile croplands cultivated for
corn and pumpkins, and its many natural
areas protected for wildlife.

Hamilton and Ipswich
APPLETON FARMS

Hamilton
APPLETON FARMS GRASS RIDES
Laid out like spokes of a wagon wheel, tree-lined carriage drives and bridle paths radiate from a central clearing called the "Roundpoint" which is marked by a large, granite pinnacle salvaged during the demolition of Gore Hall, the former Harvard College Library.

Essex

**CRANE WILDLIFE REFUGE,
THE CRANE ESTATE**

Stalks of Giant Reed (*Fragmites australis*) screen
a view from Long Island across the Castle Neck
River to the back side of Crane Beach. Though
only a small patch here, in disturbed brackish
areas, this graceful, yet aggrandizing, reed grass
can supplant native species and form large,
dense swathes offering little value to wildlife.

Ipswich

GREENWOOD FARM

The ca.1702 Paine House preserves the
ambiance of the early salt water farmstead
which operated on this upland peninsula near
the mouth of the Ipswich River. In addition to
the farm's historic interest, the surrounding
salt marsh is of great ecological importance to
a diversity of plants and animals uniquely
adapted to this habitat.

Rockport

HALIBUT POINT RESERVATION ▶
Sea swells wash over the granite edges of
Halibut Point, whose rocks and slabs have
been smoothed over the eons by the ocean's
rhythmic tide.

Rockport
HALIBUT POINT STATE PARK
Between 1895 and 1915, the Babson Farm Quarry
supplied over 1.5 million tons of granite for the
never-completed, one-mile-long Sandy Bay
Breakwater, a federal project which would have
created in Rockport's waters a 1,600-acre protected port mooring over five thousand ships. The
story of the local granite industry is told today
in the State Park's Visitor Center.

Lowell
**LOWELL NATIONAL
HISTORICAL PARK**
The industrial heritage of the "Spindle City"
is preserved and interpreted through former
textile mills, mill worker boarding houses,
and over five miles of canals. Narrated boat
tours along the Pawtucket Canal recount
the city's rapid rise as the nation's leading textile producer and its equally rapid fall at the
end of the 19th century.

North Andover
WEIR HILL

The toppled remains of this stone wall speak
of a time when the Massachusetts landscape
was largely denuded of its ancient forests to
make way for farms. Their boundaries, cropland,
and pastures were all demarcated by stone
walls, which one ox and one man could build
at a rate of just ten feet per day.

Essex
STAVROS RESERVATION

The coastal drumlin known as White's Hill rises
above the marshes of the Essex River Estuary.

Gloucester
RAVENSWOOD PARK

Lichen-covered boulders lie scattered across the
woodland floor. This serene landscape stands in
stark contrast to the destructive glacial forces
which created what we see today.

Newbury

OLD TOWN HILL

Marshland cut by snaking streams spreads
out below the western flank of Old Town Hill,
the 168-foot drumlin which early settlers called
the "Great Hill." These vast expanses of salt
marsh once provided abundant harvests of salt
marsh hay.

Beverly
LONG HILL
A horticultural orchestra of trees, shrubs, vines, herbaceous perennials, and bulbs grows in coordinated harmony in the Sedgwick Gardens at Long Hill. Laid out in a series of separate rooms, these gardens surround an antebellum-style house which serves as headquarters of The Trustees of Reservations.

Beverly
LONG HILL

Andover and North Andover
WARD RESERVATION ▶

What may at first appear to be a simple kettle hole pond is really a rare quaking bog in the process of becoming a forest. The bog's deep, cold, acidic, oxygen-poor water slows down the natural decay of dead plants which accumulate in thick mats of organic matter around the bog's edges, eventually filling it in.

Manchester-by-the-Sea
COOLIDGE RESERVATION

Salem Bay
MISERY ISLANDS
The iron hull remains of the *The City of Rockland* jut out above the waterline during low tide on Little Misery Island. The steamship was wrecked off the coast of Maine and scuttled here many years ago.

Manchester-by-the-Sea
COOLIDGE RESERVATION

Salem Bay

MISERY ISLANDS

In 1935, following a public campaign to keep
a portion of Great Misery Island from becoming
the site for an off-shore oil storage facility,
sixty-eight acres of the island were acquired
through public subscription and dedicated as
public open space.

North Andover
THE STEVENS-COOLIDGE PLACE
Formerly known as Ashdale Farm, this colonial
revivalized 18th century farmhouse overlooks
almost one hundred acres of fields, woodlands,
and formal gardens featuring lush perennial
borders, sweet-smelling old-fashioned roses,
rolling lawns, curvaceous hedges, and topiary.

Newbury
OLD TOWN HILL
The Little River glides slowly past a rocky
upland knoll before joining the much larger
Parker River on its journey out to sea.

Manchester-by-the-Sea
AGASSIZ ROCK
Agassiz Rock honors the natural historian
who theorized that the rocks that dot New
England's landscape were shaped and deposited
thousands of years ago by mile-high bodies of
advancing ice. Little Agassiz is a dramatic example of the awesome power of the glacier, which
plucked this giant boulder from bedrock and left
it propped up on the summit of Beaverdam Hill.

Beverly
MORAINE FARM
Between 1880 and 1882, Frederick Law Olmsted
designed the landscape of this 175-acre private
estate on the shore of Wenham Lake. Olmsted's
hand is evident in its separate forestry, farming,
and residential areas, winding carriage drives,
enhanced scenic vistas, and siting of buildings.
Moraine Farm is protected by a conservation
and historic preservation restriction.

Eastham
CAPE COD NATIONAL SEASHORE
Cape Cod is a glacial landscape whose light sandy soils are constantly altered by the unpredictable forces of nature. Wind and water erode cliffs, and sediments get transported down rivers and along shorelines, shrinking certain places while expanding others in a process called "longshore drift."

Cape Cod and the Islands

Rising just above the sea, the shifting landscapes of Cape Cod and the Islands—with their beaches and marshes, grasslands and moors, harbors and lighthouses—reflect the constant influence of sun, wind, and waves. Cape Cod is a low, almost flat landscape of pitch pine-oak woodlands broken here and there by small rivers, kettle hole ponds, and cranberry bogs. The ocean has built long, windswept barrier beaches that protect not only harbors but also quiet salt marshes where dune grass gives way to salt meadow grass and herons fish in the shallows. The vast expanse of the outer Cape's Atlantic beach faces the full force of the ocean. Fishing and whaling were the trades of choice in the nineteenth century, and wealthy sea captains built gracious mansions along the shore. Today, working boats still head out to sea to fish and lobster and some to study the ocean. Other boats cruise the coast and bays at leisure.

Martha's Vineyard, Nantucket, and the Elizabeth Islands have a low, rolling terrain of pitch pine-oak woods, brackish salt ponds, freshwater ponds, and, especially on Nantucket, rare fire-adapted shrubby heath and open grasslands of prairie-like plants. Except for the ridge and steep cliffs of tinted clay running along the northwest shore of Martha's Vineyard, much of the Islands' shoreline unfolds into salt marsh, salt ponds, and occasional cedar woods tucked behind dunes that line the barrier beaches. In the towns, the historic brick houses of wealthy whaling captains stand among classic, gray-shingled capes with white trim, white fences, and rose gardens. The harbors that once sent off whalers now welcome pleasure boaters and summer visitors.

Though summer beaches are crowded, there are still times and places to be alone with the sea, to hear the whispers and sighs of the quietest tides, shaping the land, shaping ourselves.

Martha's Vineyard
MYTOI
Since this Japanese-inspired garden lost over
half of its pine forest canopy to the pummeling
forces of Hurricane Bob in August 1991, it has
undergone a major transformation from an
open, shady shrub garden to one with winding
paths which lead to various distinctively
planted areas.

Martha's Vineyard
MYTOI
A gracefully arched bridge connects the tranquil
island in Mytoi Pond to the rest of the garden.

Mashpee and Sandwich
LOWELL HOLLY
Rhododendrons bloom along the mixed wood-
land peninsula of Mashpee-Wakeby Pond.

Eastham
CAPE COD NATIONAL SEASHORE
Sunrise over Coast Guard Beach.

Martha's Vineyard
WASQUE ▶
Pitch pine stands, once held in check by intense natural ground fires, now spread across the landscape in dense stands displacing increasingly rare sandplain grassland habitat. Though natural fires are now suppressed on the Islands, conservation organizations use controlled burns to achieve nature's intended balance.

Nantucket
WINDSWEPT CRANBERRY BOG
During the mid-October harvest, water reels
plow through submerged cranberry bogs,
thrashing the water around cranberry vines
until they relinquish their tart fruits. Using
large floating rings, workers gather this
buoyant crimson harvest. Berries are then
vacuumed up for transport to plants which
make sauces and jellies for Thanksgiving.

Martha's Vineyard
CAPE POGE WILDLIFE REFUGE
Red- and white-flowered rugosa roses thrive
in the windy, salt-laden air and rolling sand
dunes of many coastal landscapes, such
as Cape Poge's breathtaking barrier beach.

Martha's Vineyard
MENEMSHA HILLS
The Menemsha Hills, Vineyard Sound, and the
Chilmark coastline spread out under sunset,
absorbing and reflecting the various colors of
the visible light spectrum.

Martha's Vineyard

◄ GAY HEAD CLIFFS

Declared a National Natural Landmark in 1965, these dramatic escarpments rise one hundred feet above the surf and contain in their prehistoric strata fossil-bearing sediments deposited here by the glaciers. Conservation land surrounds Gay Head Light, which, since 1799, has warned ships away from a submerged chain of offshore boulders known as the Devil's Bridge.

Nantucket

COSKATA-COATUE
WILDLIFE REFUGE

Rebuilt in 1985 following its collapse into the sea the year before, the current Great Point Lighthouse is the third such beacon to stand on the tip of Nantucket's longest barrier beach.

Nantucket
COATUE POINT
Sunset over the town of Nantucket as seen from
Coatue Point across Nantucket Harbor.

Falmouth

ASHUMET HOLLY

Grassy Pond is a splendid example of a kettle
hole pond, formed approximately ten thousand
years ago when a giant chunk of ice was left
behind during the glacial retreat. The ice melted,
forming a deep kettle-shaped basin which is
not fed or drained by a stream, but entirely
dependent on the level of ground water and
rainfall in its watershed.

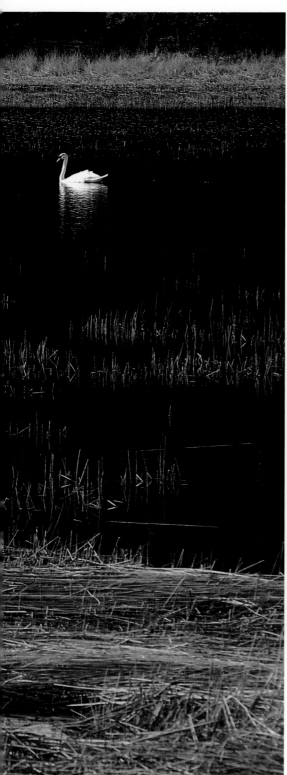

Mashpee

MASHPEE RIVER RESERVATION

The banks of this five-mile river, which begins
at Mashpee-Wakeby Pond and empties into
Pirate's Cove on Popponnesset Bay, are almost
entirely protected from source to mouth. Its
clean waters make Mashpee River one of the
finest brook trout streams on Cape Cod.

CAPE COD NATIONAL SEASHORE
Through an Act of Congress approved by
President Kennedy in 1961, the Cape Cod
National Seashore became a reality. It protects
forty miles of Cape Cod's pristine shoreline
and 43,600 acres of dunes, marshes, ponds,
and forests. Each year, five million people enjoy
its eleven nature trails, three bike paths, and
six swimming, fishing, and wind-surfing
beaches.

Royalston
DOANE'S FALLS
While the rest of nature is locked in
winter's frozen grip, the persistent waters
of Doane's Falls slip through in an act of
proud defiance.

Central Massachusetts

The rivers of the central uplands course through a rolling land of rich woodlands, family farms and orchards, small New England villages, and factory towns. Here, the coastal plain ends, and the granite backbone of the uplands emerges to form a rugged landscape of hills, low mountains, rock ledges, and outcrops, anchored by 2,006-foot-high Mount Wachusett. These higher elevations produce a forest of birch, beech, and sugar maple as well as white pine, oak, and black spruce. Beneath the trees, old stonewalls and cellar holes stand witness to a time when farming flourished. Bogs, lakes, and beaver ponds abound.

The major rivers of this region — the Nashua, Millers, Chicopee, Quinebaug, Swift, and Blackstone — splash and tumble over ledges and rocks forming waterfalls and quiet pools. For centuries, the rivers worked. First harnessed by Yankee farmers to run saw- and gristmills in the 1700s, the rivers soon powered the new cotton milling industry. Later still, they ran factories during the heyday of manufacturing when Worcester, Gardner, and smaller towns produced cotton and wool, chairs and clocks, and wooden rocking horses.

Today, the rivers run alongside small town centers where the town common is flanked by white churches and grange halls and often adorned with a bandstand awaiting summer concerts. Outside the towns, farm fields, woodlots, and orchards cover the hills. Apple trees fill the air with fragrant blossoms in spring and fill bushel baskets with tangy fruit in fall. Some wilder places endure. The lands of the Quabbin Reservoir and many other woodlands are large and remote enough that there's a good chance to see turkeys slip among the trees, hear barred owls hooting softly at twilight, and witness a bald eagle swoop low to snatch a fish from sparkling blue waters.

West Brookfield
ROCK HOUSE RESERVATION
The region's glacial history comes alive in the form of massive granite boulders which wade along the shores of the reflective Carter Pond. The property's overhanging rock shelter, used by Native Americans as a winter hunting camp, gives the reservation its peculiar name.

Royalston
JACOBS HILL
A short hike up Jacobs Hill to its open ridge rewards one's efforts with a view, three hundred feet below, of the primeval Tully River Basin and its colorful red maple swamp.

Petersham
BROOKS WOODLAND PRESERVE
Patience, planning, and perseverance are
hallmarks of the character of the industrious
beaver.

West Brookfield
ROCK HOUSE RESERVATION
Following a concerted effort in the 1940s
to reintroduce beavers into Massachusetts,
these ingenious, sometimes pesky, rodents
have made a tremendous comeback after
being trapped almost to the point of extinction during the 19th century.

Petersham
BROOKS WOODLAND PRESERVE ▶
Though almost unimaginable today, the groves
of white pines that characterize this forest
landscape belie its agrarian past. These lands
were once cleared as pastures for pioneer
farmsteads whose foundations and cellar holes
are found throughout the Preserve.

Royalston

DOANE'S FALLS

Early spring snow melt hastens the flow of
Lawrence Brook through its sinuous freshwater
marshes. Before reaching its destination in Tully
Lake, these waters tumble almost two hundred
feet in a series of great falls whose energy was
once harnessed to power mills for grain, lumber,
textiles, and wooden pails and tubs.

Petersham
HARVARD FOREST
Daybreak over Connor's Pond on the fringe
of a 3,000-acre mixed hardwood and conifer
research forest. Nearby, the Fisher Museum
presents two dozen three-dimensional diora-
mas portraying the history, management,
and ecology of central New England forests.

Leominster
DOYLE ESTATE
A Giverny-style arched foot bridge leads to a shaded island in a farm pond. The nearby hayfield is part of a larger estate, nestled between the growing twin cities of Leominster and Fitchburg, which will one day become a public reservation.

Petersham
SWIFT RIVER RESERVATION
For a fleeting moment in autumn, hay-scented ferns, which colonize illuminated openings in the woodland floor, turn hues of yellow and gold before browning under the harsh cold of winter.

Petersham
SWIFT RIVER RESERVATION ▶
The Swift River often slows down during the
dry summer months, revealing in its exposed
river bed a secret, perhaps unexpected, landscape with a beauty all its own.

Petersham
BROOKS WOODLAND PRESERVE
Stalwart trees strain under the weight of
heavy snow, dipping into the frozen waters
of Moccasin Brook.

Princeton and Westminster
WACHUSETT MOUNTAIN
From the 2,000-foot summit of Wachusett
Mountain, the early evening sun flashes off the
surface of Wachusett Lake as dusk settles over
the Leominster State Forest.

New Salem and Royalston
**BEAR'S DEN, DOANE'S FALLS,
ROYALSTON FALLS**
Both beautiful and utilitarian, Central Massa-
chusetts waterfalls such as these supported
active mill operations during generations past.
Today, they are appreciated by a generation
seeking opportunities for quiet contemplation.

Princeton
WACHUSETT MEADOW
Floating leaves of autumn provide one of the
season's many artistic delights along the shores
of this 200-acre beaver pond at the base of
Wachusett Mountain.

116

Harvard
CARLSON ORCHARDS
The legendary Johnny Appleseed was born in Central Massachusetts, and apple orchards remain an important part of the region's landscape character. Towns in the Nashoba Valley are well known for their orchards, many of which offer popular pick-your-own opportunities, including Carlson Orchards, now protected by an agricultural preservation restriction.

Sturbridge
TANTIUSQUES
Used by the Nipmuck as a source for ceremonial paint, this graphite shaft became the site of a colonial mining operation in 1644. Its "black lead" was later used in the manufacture of pencils and crucibles.

QUABBIN RESERVOIR ▶

In 1936, following a controversial search for
a site for a new water reservoir for Boston-
area residents, the 95,000-acre watershed con-
taining the now-lost towns of Dana, Enfield,
Greenwich, and Prescott was chosen. The Swift
River was impounded in 1939 and, seven years
later, a 412-billion-gallon reservoir covering
thirty-nine square miles was filled to the brim.

Northbridge and Uxbridge
BLACKSTONE RIVER AND CANAL
Visitors can walk along the towpath or canoe
through restored sections of this canal which,
during the 1830s and 40s, transported raw
materials and manufactured goods between
Worcester and Providence. Designed to elimi-
nate the expense of overland transport to and
from Boston, the canal was itself made redun-
dant by the railroad just two decades after the
canal's completion.

Royalston

ROYALSTON FALLS

Before plunging seventy feet over Royalston
Falls, Falls Brook swirls through a rocky ravine,
continually carving out holes in the bedrock,
leaving behind miniature stone bridges span-
ning the stream bed.

Williamstown
FIELD FARM
The grand scale of the Greylock Range dwarfs
a small herd of dairy cows.

Connecticut River Valley and the Berkshires

The view from the top of Mount Holyoke reveals a great New England river meandering through its broad, flat flood plain. It winds past remnant stands of flood plain forest; farm fields growing cabbage, corn, and tobacco; pastures of dairy cows; small towns and cities; and bustling college campuses. First, Native Americans and, then, successive waves of immigrants arrived here to till the rich soil. Along the river at Turners Falls, Holyoke, and Springfield, the river was harnessed to run nineteenth-century mills that produced cotton, wool, and paper during the Industrial Revolution. The cities continued as centers for manufacturing and business. Now, through fishways at dams, they lend a hand to the river so that when the shadbush blooms in spring, the fishes for which it is named can make their way past waterfalls and other barriers and return to their natal streams to spawn.

West of the valley, the Hoosic, Housatonic, Westfield, and Deerfield rivers wind and plummet through a rugged country that harbors among its hills elegant estates and rustic sugar houses, concert halls for music and dance, and bobcats and bears. From 3,491-foot-high Mount Greylock, the Berkshire hills roll across the land covered in forests of maple, birch, beech, and oak with patches of spruce-fir woods. Here are the marble valleys, where limestone rock produces sweet, alkaline soils rich in calcium that nourish rare ferns and wildflowers. From river valley to ridge top, the Appalachian Trail marks a quiet path across the land. The nineteenth-century summer homes of wealthy families from Boston and New York stand alongside the simpler homes of the hill towns, where life revolves around the spring sugaring season, the summer planting season, and the fall harvest season when the hills glow red, orange, green, and gold.

Sheffield

BARTHOLOMEW'S COBBLE

The unusual alkaline soils of this National
Natural Landmark support a wide diversity of
plants, including over five hundred wildflowers
and a remarkable concentration of over fifty
fern species and their allies.

Sheffield

BARTHOLOMEW'S COBBLE

Along its course in the south Berkshires, the Housatonic River flows past broad riverside meadows and marshes of these alluvial bottomlands. Weathered limestone cobbles, which give the reservation its name, rise starkly above the river on its western shores.

Deerfield
OLD DEERFIELD
The Pocumtuck Ridge overlooks the old
village of Deerfield, its Common, distinguished
Academy, and nearly 1,000 acres of rich farmland. Sixteen 18th- and 19th-century museum
houses and a display archive of over 50,000
objects of early New England life are part and
parcel of this meticulously preserved, quintes-
sential New England town.

Sheffield
SCHENOB BROOK FEN
As part of a state-listed Area of Critical Environmental Concern, this nature preserve protects a section of southern New England's largest and finest calcareous wetland system. Its unusual calcium-rich bedrock confers alkalinity to its soils, supporting rare or threatened species of plants including many orchids, grasses, and sedges.

Deerfield
MOUNT SUGARLOAF ►
Viewed from the top of South Sugarloaf Mountain, named for the hill's sandstone rock called Sugarloaf Arkose, the broad agricultural landscape of the Connecticut River Valley spreads out below with the Holyoke Range forming the distant horizon.

Windsor

NOTCHVIEW

Classic cross-country skiers enjoy Notchview's
seventeen kilometers of groomed trails, many
of which pass through these deep plantations
of Norway spruce, planted in the 1930s by
Colonel A. D. Budd as an experiment in forestry.

Windsor

NOTCHVIEW

Several old roads still traverse the three thousand now-forested acres of Notchview. These roads provided vital links for early inhabitants who settled the over fifty farms and homesteads which today comprise the reservation. They grazed cattle and sheep and cultivated crops. Some made a living through lumbering, charcoal making, and axe manufacturing.

Stockbridge
NAUMKEAG
Long before the Choate family purchased
this site on Prospect Hill, during summers
throughout the 1870s, they enjoyed its
pastoral fields and mountain views. Their
love of the outdoors and country life is
reflected in the way they landscaped their
grounds, planted their gardens, and
designed their gabled mansion.

Stockbridge
NAUMKEAG
The Chinese Garden, seen through the round
Moon Gate, and the Blue Steps were two of
Fletcher Steele's many ingenious designs for
the gardens at Naumkeag.

Sheffield

BARTHOLOMEW'S COBBLE ▶

Each autumn, birds of prey depend on mountain ranges and valleys to guide their migratory flight path. As seen from Hurlburt's Hill, the Taconic Range and the Housatonic River Basin are important "leading lines" used by eagles, hawks, falcons, and kestrels during their annual migration.

Stockbridge
THE MISSION HOUSE
After living with Mahican Indians in a mission he had established in Stockbridge, John Sergeant built this house on Prospect Hill following his marriage in 1739. In 1926–27, it was disassembled, restored, and rebuilt on its present location only a lot removed from the site of the original mission. Fletcher Steele designed its garden in the "colonial" manner.

Tyringham
TYRINGHAM COBBLE
Beyond the town cemetery, the Appalachian
Trail passes over Tyringham Cobble. Since the
cobble's rock strata are identical to those of
Backbone Mountain, and since the rocks on the
cobble's ridge are older than those at its base,
many believe that Tyringham Cobble broke off
of Backbone Mountain and flipped over in a
massive geologic cataclysm.

Windsor

NOTCHVIEW

As the autumn days shorten, an arsenal
of maple, birch, beech, cherry, ash, and tupelo
explode in Notchview's annual fall foliage
extravaganza.

Otis and Tyringham
McLENNAN RESERVATION
The waters of Hale Swamp reflect the fiery glow
of bordering maples.

Chesterfield
CHESTERFIELD GORGE ▶
While calm most of the year, the waters of
the Westfield River swell during the annual
spring thaw. The river has rushed for thousands
of years through Chesterfield Gorge, carving
a steep, narrow chasm through solid granite
bedrock.

Ashfield
BEAR SWAMP
The western brow of Ridge Hill provides a
panoramic view of seasonal changes in nearby
Apple Valley and upon the distant slopes of
Vermont's Green Mountains.

Otis and Tyringham
McLENNAN RESERVATION
Dead and decaying tree trunks are tell-tale
signs of the always busy beaver. Over many
years, they have transformed a trickling tribu-
tary of Hop Brook into a sprawling beaver
swamp at the foot of Round Mountain.

Ashfield
CHAPELBROOK
Within an otherwise silent landscape, hearing
the distant sound of a brook cascading in a
series of waterfalls beckons the explorer hidden
inside all of us.

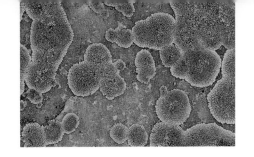

Tyringham
COLUMNS OF ASHINTULLY
Between 1910 and 1912, Egyptologist Robb de Peyster Tytus built for his new bride a white, 35-room Georgian-style mansion overlooking the southern end of Tyringham Valley. Tragically, it was destroyed by fire in 1952. Only the front terrace, foundation, and four Doric columns of the great mansion remain today as romantic ruins for visitors to explore.

Cummington

**THE WILLIAM CULLEN
BRYANT HOMESTEAD**

The great 19th-century poet, journalist, and statesman began and ended his communion with nature here. In 1865, he bought back his boyhood home and made it, for the remaining years of his life, a beloved summer retreat. The sugar maples that he planted along the carriage drive—and the memory of his life's work—live on today.

Great Barrington
MONUMENT MOUNTAIN ▶
The size of the reservation on this south
Berkshire sentinel is nearly double what it was
when established over a hundred years ago.
When its integrity was threatened by a pro-
posal to build a 200-unit mountainside condo-
minium complex, local townspeople rallied to
oppose the project and raise the funds needed
to purchase the land from the developer.

Williamstown
PARADISE FARM
Hay harvesting in the fields of Paradise Farm,
a private farm protected by an agricultural
preservation restriction.

Hadley and South Hadley
MOUNT HOLYOKE
Mount Holyoke is a well-known marker on
the horizon of farms in the Connecticut River
Valley. Despite the mountain's own preservation,
much of the productive agricultural landscape
it watches over remains vulnerable to development.

Williamstown
FIELD FARM

Williamstown
FIELD FARM
Field Farm's extensive cornfields are just one
of its many pleasures.

North Adams
MOUNT GREYLOCK ▶
Will our propensity to impose dominion over
the landscape be the inheritance we leave to
our children and our children's children?

Thanks to enormous private generosity and a long tradition of public commitment to conservation, over twenty percent of the state has been protected from development. Richard Cheek's marvelous photographs pay a lasting tribute to this impressive achievement. Though less well-known than the American Revolution, the public high school, or Boston baked beans, leadership in conservation has been one of Massachusetts' most important contributions to the nation. However, given today's population, the conserved landscapes of the Commonwealth amount to only one-sixth of an acre of open space per resident—not our idea of elbow room.

Massachusetts residents live in one of the most densely populated states in the nation. We currently enjoy the fruits of a robust economy that promises long-term economic expansion, but, from Provincetown to Williamstown, the economic boom portends development at a rate that greatly exceeds population growth. Many self-contained communities, their compact village centers set apart by stretches of woods and farmland, are being transformed into commuter suburbs. Their once scenic roads are choked with traffic, their open lands now posted, and their municipal services stretched to capacity. This relentless sprawl blots the scenery that is our window to the landscape, fragmenting wildlife habitat and severing the threads—the trails and paths—that connect our communities to the natural world.

While the special places portrayed in this book are protected, too many of them remain as small, isolated gems in an increasingly tarnished and battered setting, their vistas vulnerable to development. With the ecological, scenic, and historic integrity of the landscape in jeopardy, private groups and public agencies in Massachusetts must unite in an ambitious and coordinated effort. Landowners must be encouraged to preserve their property through various techniques and incentives. Three current reports—*Conserving our Common Wealth* by The Trustees of Reservations; *Losing Ground* by the Massachusetts Audubon Society; and *Our Irreplaceable Heritage* by the Natural Heritage & Endangered Species Program, the Massachusetts Division of Fisheries & Wildlife, and the Massachusetts Chapter of The Nature Conservancy—call for the protection of large, unbroken reserves of open space. Wherever possible, these reserves should be linked together by broad corridors of protected land. Every community, indeed every person, in the Commonwealth should have ready access to a network of conservation land.

This vision can still be achieved, but, in the face of escalating land values and development pressures, time is running out. We have an all-too-brief opportunity to save additional open space, especially in blocks large enough to support a diversity of plants and animals or to preserve the distinctive character of our communities. The work we do in our generation will critically impact the ultimate fate of the landscape of Massachusetts and its accessibility to the public.

Guided by the vision of Charles Eliot, and inspired by the conservation successes so vividly represented by these photographs, The Trustees of Reservations—now under the leadership of Andrew Kendall—will continue to work to secure an enriched legacy of protected land for Massachusetts. I join Andy in inviting you to support The Trustees of Reservations and its many conservation colleagues in this effort.

FREDERIC WINTHROP
Executive Director, January 1985–March 2000
The Trustees of Reservations

About The Trustees of Reservations

WHO WE ARE

The Trustees of Reservations is a member-supported nonprofit [501(c)3] organization formed for charitable purposes to preserve, for public use and enjoyment, landscapes of exceptional scenic, historic, and ecological value in Massachusetts and to protect special places across the state. The organization was founded in 1891 by a small group of open space visionaries led by landscape architect Charles Eliot, a protégé of Frederick Law Olmsted. Witnessing the dramatic loss to development of large amounts of land in the Boston metropolitan area, this group successfully campaigned for the establishment of what became the first private, statewide conservation and preservation organization in the nation.

WHAT WE DO

The Trustees of Reservations works to enhance and extend the Commonwealth's system of protected lands through acquisition of new reservations and lands associated with existing reservations, conservation restrictions on private land, landowner assistance, statewide planning, collaboration, and legislative advocacy.

Management of reservations is guided by a three-fold commitment to protecting scenic, historic, and ecological resources, providing public access, and maintaining a high quality visitor experience. Natural resource protection is achieved through inventory, monitoring, and research, habitat conservation and management, habitat restoration, and rare species protection. Protection of cultural resources entails research, preservation, exhibition, and interpretation of historic buildings, structures, landscape features, and fine and decorative arts.

The Trustees of Reservations uses a comprehensive mapping and management planning framework to locate, identify, and describe the natural and cultural resources to be conserved at each reservation. Using management standards and guidelines, each reservation is then specifically managed to protect these resources and, at the same time, provide compatible forms of public access and use.

WHAT WE PROTECT AND WHY

The Trustees of Reservations conserves almost 35,000 acres of land across the state comprising over eighty reservations and approximately two hundred parcels of private land on which the organization holds conservation restrictions.

These landscapes are diverse and include hills, mountains, and ridges; forests and woodlands; lakes, ponds, and bogs; river gorges, waterfalls, and floodplains; islands, rocky coastline, beaches, and sand dunes; marshes, grasslands, heath, and swamp; farms and agricultural land; prehistoric and relic industrial sites; and historic houses, designed landscapes, and gardens. Four reservations are National Historic Landmarks; eight are on the National Register of Historic Places; and one is on the National Registry of Natural Landmarks. Eleven provide links in the Bay Circuit Trail, Appalachian Trail, Mid-State Trail, and Metacomet-Monadnock Trail.

Together, these reservations offer a wide range of recreational opportunities, such as bird-watching, nature study, canoeing and kayaking, boating and sailing, cross-country skiing, snow shoeing, fishing, hiking, horseback riding, picnicking, swimming, pond skating, and tours. Over two hundred public events, programs, and activities are held year-round. Several reservations offer overnight B&B accommodation and can be rented for meetings and functions.

Through their cultural and natural history, the conserved landscapes of The Trustees of Reservations tell the story of the interaction of people and land in what we today call Massachusetts. The organization produces a wide range of publications and maintains a web site to help visitors explore and interpret these sites. We believe that those who enjoy and draw inspiration from our reservations and understand our mission will become stewards with us in protecting additional special places across the state.

HOW WE ARE SUPPORTED

As a nonprofit organization, we rely for support entirely upon membership dues, contributions, grants, reservation receipts, special events, and endowments. We enjoy the support of hundreds of volunteers and approximately 25,000 members who live in Massachusetts, other parts of New England and the USA, and several countries abroad.

The Trustees
of Reservations

List of Photographed Sites

Private Conservation Groups and Public Agencies

Nantucket; **Lowell Holly**, Mashpee and Sandwich; **Mashpee River Reservation**, Mashpee; **Menemsha Hills**, Chilmark, Martha's Vineyard; **Mytoi**, Chappaquiddick, Martha's Vineyard; **Wasque**, Chappaquiddick, Martha's Vineyard

Other sites:

Ashumet Holly Wildlife Sanctuary, Falmouth (MAS); **Cape Cod National Seashore**, Eastham (NPS); **Coatue Point**, Nantucket (Nonprofit); **Gay Head Cliffs**, Aquinnah, Martha's Vineyard (Private, Non-profit, Town); **Windswept Cranberry Bog**, Nantucket (Nonprofit)

CENTRAL MASSACHUSETTS

Properties of The Trustees of Reservations:

Bear's Den, New Salem; **Brooks Woodland Preserve**, Petersham; **Doane's Falls**, Royalston; **Doyle Estate**, Leominster; **Jacobs Hill**, Royalston; **Rock House Reservation**, West Brookfield; **Royalston Falls**, Royalston; **Swift River Reservation**, Petersham; **Tantiusques**, Sturbridge

Other sites:

Blackstone River and Canal State Heritage Park, Northbridge and Uxbridge (DEM); **Carlson Orchards**, Harvard (Private); **Harvard Forest**, Petersham (Harvard University); **Quabbin Reservoir**, Belchertown (MDC); **Wachusett Meadow Wildlife Sanctuary**, Princeton (MAS); **Wachusett Mountain State Reservation**, Princeton and Westminster (DEM)

CONNECTICUT RIVER VALLEY AND THE BERKSHIRES

Properties of The Trustees of Reservations:

Columns of Ashintully, Tyringham; **Bartholomew's Cobble**, Sheffield; **Bear Swamp**, Ashfield; **The William Cullen Bryant Homestead**, Cummington; **Chapelbrook**, Ashfield; **Chesterfield Gorge**, Chesterfield; **Field Farm**, Williamstown; **McLennan Reservation**, Otis and Tyringham; **The Mission House**, Stockbridge; **Monument Mountain**, Great Barrington; **Naumkeag**, Stockbridge; **Notchview**, Windsor; **Tyringham Cobble**, Tyringham

Other sites:

Mount Greylock State Reservation, Lanesborough (DEM); **Mount Holyoke, Skinner State Park**, Hadley and South Hadley (DEM); **Mount Sugarloaf State Reservation**, Deerfield (DEM); **Old Deerfield**, Deerfield (Private, Town); **Paradise Farm**, Williamstown (Private); **Schenob Brook Fen**, Sheffield (TNC)

Statewide or national groups involved in land stewardship or acquisition in Massachusetts:

PRIVATE

American Farmland Trust
1200 18th Street, NW
Washington, DC 20036
(202) 331-7300
www.farmland.org

Appalachian Mountain Club
5 Joy Street
Boston, MA 02108
(617) 523-0636
www.outdoors.org

The Conservation Fund
1800 N. Kent Street
Arlington, VA 22209
(703) 525-6300
www.conservationfund.org

The Garden Conservancy
P. O. Box 219
Cold Spring, NY 10516
(914) 265-5384
www.gardenconservancy.org

Historic Massachusetts
45 School Street
Boston, MA 02108
(617) 723-3383
www.historicmass.org

Land Trust Alliance
1319 F Street, NW
Washington, DC 20004
(202) 638-4725
www.lta.org

Massachusetts Audubon Society (MAS)
208 South Great Road
Lincoln, MA 01773
(800) AUDUBON (283-8266)
www.massaudubon.org

Massachusetts Land Trust Coalition
www2.shore.net/~mltc
Information about local and regional land trusts and conservation organizations

Massachusetts Watershed Coalition
www.ultranet.com/~mwc
Information about local and regional watershed councils and associations

National Trust for Historic Preservation, Northeast Regional Office
7 Faneuil Hall Marketplace
Boston, MA 02109
(617) 523-0885
www.nationaltrust.org

The Nature Conservancy, Massachusetts Chapter (TNC)
79 Milk Street
Boston, MA 02109
(617) 423-2545
www.tnc.org

New England Forestry Foundation
283 Old Dunstable Road
Groton, MA 01450
(978) 448-8380
www.neforestry.org

Society for the Preservation of New England Antiquities
141 Cambridge Street
Boston, MA 02114
(617) 227-3956
www.spnea.org

Trout Unlimited
1500 Wilson Boulevard
Arlington, VA 22209
(703) 522-0200
www.tu.org

Trust for Public Land, New England Regional Office
33 Union Street
Boston, MA 02108
(617) 367-6200
www.igc.apc.org/tpl/nearu/
nero/index.html

The Trustees of Reservations
572 Essex Street
Beverly, MA 01915
(978) 921-1944
www.thetrustees.org

PUBLIC

Executive Office of Environmental Affairs
100 Cambridge Street
Boston, MA 02202
(617) 727-9800
www.state.ma.us/envir/eoea.htm

Massachusetts Department of Environmental Management (DEM)
100 Cambridge Street
Boston, MA 02202
(617) 626-1250
www.magnet.state.ma.us/dem/
dem.htm

Massachusetts Division of Fisheries, Wildlife, and Environmental Law Enforcement
100 Cambridge Street
Boston, MA 02202
(617) 626-1591
www.magnet.state.ma.us/dfwele

Massachusetts Department of Food and Agriculture (DFA)
100 Cambridge Street
Boston, MA 02202
(617) 626-1700
www.massdfa.org

Massachusetts Historical Commission
220 Morrissey Boulevard
Boston, MA 02125
(617) 727-8470
www.magnet.state.ma.us/sec/
mhc/mhcidx.htm

Metropolitan District Commission (MDC)
20 Somerset Street
Boston, MA 02108
(617) 727-5215
www.magnet.state.ma.us/mdc/
mdc_home.htm

National Park Service, Boston Support Office (NPS)
15 State Street
Boston, MA 02109
(617) 223-5123
www.nps.gov

US Fish and Wildlife Service
300 Westgate Center Drive
Hadley, MA 01035
(413) 253-8200
www.northeast.fws.gov/ma.htm

For information about other private and public conservation groups, visit the "Conservation Connections" resource pages on The Trustees of Reservations' web site, www.thetrustees.org.

References

TRAVEL GUIDES

Ahern, Jack. *A Guide to the Landscape Architecture of Boston.* Cambridge, MA: Hubbard Educational Trust, 1999.

Appalachian Mountain Club. *AMC Massachusetts & Rhode Island Travel Guide.* Boston, MA: Appalachian Mountain Club Books, 1995.

Appalachian Mountain Club. *AMC Quiet Water Canoe Guide: Massachusetts/Connecticut/Rhode Island.* Boston, MA: Appalachian Mountain Club Books, 1993.

Appalachian Mountain Club. A*MC River Guide: Massachusetts/Connecticut/Rhode Island.* Boston, MA: Appalachian Mountain Club Books, 1991.

Brady, John, and White, Brian. *Fifty Hikes in Massachusetts.* Woodstock, VT: Backcountry Publications, 1992.

Cuyler, Lewis C. *Bike Rides in the Berkshire Hills.* Lee, MA: Berkshire House, 1995.

Finch, Robert. *The Smithsonian Guide to Natural America. Southern New England: Massachusetts, Connecticut and Rhode Island.* Washington, DC: Smithsonian Books and New York, NY: Random House, 1996.

Grant, K. *Cape Cod and the Islands: An Explorer's Guide.* Woodstock, VT: The Countryman Press, 1995.

Jane, Nancy. *Bicycle Touring in the Pioneer Valley.* Amherst, MA: University of Massachusetts Press, 1995.

Kulik, Stephen, et. al. *The Audubon Society Field Guide to the Natural Places of the Northeast: Coastal.* New York, NY: Pantheon, 1984.

Kulik, Stephen, et. al. *The Audubon Society Field Guide to the Natural Places of the Northeast: Inland.* New York, NY: Pantheon, 1984.

Laubach, René. *A Guide to Natural Places in the Berkshire Hills.* Lee, MA: Berkshire House, 1992.

Massachusetts Audubon Society. *Guide to Wildlife Sanctuaries, Nature Centers, and Policy Offices.* Lincoln, MA: Massachusetts Audubon Society.

Massachusetts Coastal Zone Management. *Massachusetts Coast Guide.* Boston, MA: Massachusetts Coastal Zone Management, 1995.

Massachusetts Department of Environmental Management. *Massachusetts Forests and Parks: A Guide to Recreation.* Boston, MA: Massachusetts Department of Environmental Management, 1999.

McAdow, Ron. *The Charles River: Exploring Nature and History on Foot and by Canoe.* Marlborough, MA: Bliss, 1992.

Metropolitan District Commission; Griffin, Susan; and DelVecchio, Leanne. *MDC Reservations and Facilities Guide.* Boston, MA: Metropolitan District Commission.

Perk, Jeff. *Massachusetts Handbook.* Chico, CA: Moon Publications, 1998.

Perry, John, and Perry, Jane G. *The Sierra Club Guide to the Natural Areas of New England.* San Francisco, CA: Sierra Club Books, 1997.

Sinai, Lee. *Exploring in and around Boston on Bike and Foot.* Boston, MA: Appalachian Mountain Club Books, 1996.

Society for the Preservation of New England Antiquities. *SPNEA Guide.* Boston, MA: Society for the Preservation of New England Antiquities.

Stevens, Lauren R. *Hikes & Walks in the Berkshire Hills.* Lee, MA: Berkshire House, 1990.

Stone, Howard. *Short Bike Rides/Eastern Massachusetts.* Chester, CT: Globe Pequot Press, 1997.

Stone, Howard. *Short Bike Rides/Western Massachusetts.* Chester, CT: Globe Pequot Press, 1997.

The Trustees of Reservations, and Hopkins, Libby Ola. *The Trustees of Reservations Property Guide.* Beverly, MA: The Trustees of Reservations, 1996.

Tougias, Michael. *Exploring the Hidden Charles: A Guide to Outdoor Activities on Boston's Celebrated River.* Boston, MA: Appalachian Mountain Club Books, 1997.

Tougias, Michael, and René Laubach. *Nature Walks in Central Massachusetts.* Boston, MA: Appalachian Mountain Club Books, 1996.

Tougias, Michael. *Nature Walks in Eastern Massachusetts.* Boston, MA: Appalachian Mountain Club Books, 1993.

Tree, Christina, and Davis, W. *Massachusetts: An Explorer's Guide.* Woodstock, VT: The Countryman Press, 1996.

LAND CONSERVATION REPORTS AND TECHNICAL GUIDES

Barbour, H. T.; Simmons, P. Swain; and Woolsey, H. *Our Irreplaceable Heritage: Protecting Biodiversity in Massachusetts.* Boston, MA: Natural Heritage & Endangered Species Program, Division of Fisheries & Wildlife, and the Massachusetts Chapter of The Nature Conservancy, [1998].

Massachusetts Executive Office of Environmental Affairs. *Enhancing the Future of the Metropolitan Park System, Final Report and Recommendations of the Green Ribbon Commission.* Boston, Massachusetts: Massachusetts Executive Office of Environmental Affairs, [1996].

Massachusetts Executive Office of Environmental Affairs. *The View from Borderland, Report of the Governor's Blue Ribbon Panel on Land Protection.* Boston, MA: Massachusetts Executive Office of Environmental Affairs, [1998].

Steel, J. *Losing Ground (Second Edition): An Analysis of Recent Rates and Patterns of Development and Their Effects on Open Space in Massachusetts.* Lincoln, MA: Massachusetts Audubon Society, [1999].

The Trustees of Reservations. *Conserving our Commonwealth: A Vision for the Massachusetts Landscape.* Beverly, MA: The Trustees of Reservations, [1999].

Ward, W., ed. *Land Conservation Options: A Guide for Massachusetts Landowners.* Beverly, MA: Essex County Greenbelt Association and The Trustees of Reservations, [1998].

OTHER

Cronon, W., ed. *Uncommon Ground: Rethinking the Human Place in Nature.* New York, New York: W.W. Norton & Co., 1996.

Eliot, Charles W. *Charles Eliot, Landscape Architect.* With a new introduction by Keith N. Morgan. Amherst, MA: University of Massachusetts Press, in association with Library of American Landscape History, 1999.

Foster, Charles H.W., ed. *Stepping Back to Look Forward: A History of the Massachusetts Forest.* Cambridge, MA: Harvard University Press, 1998.

Jorgensen, N. A *Guide to New England's Landscape.* Chester, Connecticut: The Globe Pequot Press, 1977.

Leahy, C.; Mitchell, J. H.; and Conuel, T. *The Nature of Massachusetts.* Reading, Massachusetts: Addison-Wesley, 1996.

McCullough, Robert. *The Landscape of Community: A History of Communal Forests in New England.* Hanover, NH: University Press of New England, 1995.

Morgan, Keith N. *Charles Eliot 1859–1897 Held in Trust: Charles Eliot's Vision for the New England Landscape.* Bethesda, Maryland: National Association for Olmsted Parks, 1991.

Wessels, Tom. *Reading the Forested Landscape: A Natural History of New England.* Woodstock, VT: Countryman Press, 1997.